Falling in Love
at
36

Falling in Love

at

36

Breska Liotson

For G. K. R. Crawford

For J. W. B.

For the heartbroken

CONTENTS

Falling in Love
at
36

The Words

This is my love letter to you
The words I chose carefully
To express my feelings of love & trust
The words I chose for you

These words are my love song for you
A swan song to my solo life
Because even if you say no
I'll still sing just for you

I am below your balcony calling
Professing my feelings for you
Telling the story of my heart
Waiting to catch a glimpse of your face

As I say these words aloud
I confess the truth inside me
The way my heart beats for you
And how I've awaited this feeling

Finally not least of all
I say the words that mean everything
The poetry of my heartstrings
Until at last the truth is known

Daily Poetry

Dawn

I used to keep from seeing the sun
rising before the day began
the world turning slowly and yearning
the tired night settling to day

Now I wake to the fresh air
the light barely peeking over the horizon
rising to the kiss of dew
and chasing the dreams in the night

I fight for my dreams in the morning
no shadows to hide from my dreams
as I face my fears on the ice surface
the sun begins to peek and to wave

Soulless

what do I do with heartless friend
or soulless enemy
or one from whom I can no longer defend

what do I do with the changes coming fast
or the pain that keeps going
or this darkness that swells up from my past

what do I do with the cold
or the chill from the friend who is not
or the love lost in the times of old

what do I do with this place
or battlefield of pain
or world without a kind look on your face

I find a way to carry on
in the face of your soulless self

Mind

Do I mind
That you are on my mind
That my thoughts are filled with you
Do I mind
That I hear your voice in my head
That you are near though you are far from me
Do I mind
That I carry you with me
That you are here in my heart
Do I mind?

I mind the absence of you
I mind the silence when your voice is far
When you are in another room or another place
I mind the un-view of your face

I do not mind being alone
I do not mind the solitude
But you are with me in my life
And I mind the space between us
I mind the time apart
I mind, but do not mind that
I can be patient
Especially for you

Do I mind?
Yes
I mind the distance between us
I mind that you are on my mind
I mind being away from you
I will always mind

Alone

What does it mean to be alone again
After all the time that I've been here
with you in this life
Where do we go from here
when there is no "we" to go with
and the life I thought I knew
comes to its close
almost forgotten

but how do I learn
to live my life

as it once was when it was just me

Do I know the answers to these questions?
Do you?

Halfway

When I can't make the journey
And time is not on my side
Meet me halfway

When you long to see me
But I am stranded in my life
Meet me halfway

When the journey becomes too much
And everyone leaves again
Meet me halfway

When the world gets too crowded
But you long for my company
Meet me halfway

Text

tone and tumble
and turpentine
and torpor
texting by testing
tempting
trialing
thrice the trouble
targeting my truth
taking me towards
tumbling
torment
to times
testing the trite
testing the tense
testing the temperate
testing the truth
truth in targets
targets in trust
testing in texting
to tempt the take
taking the time
to think
.
.
.

then texting

Credit

I just keep pretending that I'm financially fine
That I have money in the bank to spare
And I'm not just running on fumes for this year.
I just keep pretending,
As if it's all ok,
And I'll be fine someday.
But really I keep using my cards,
Throwing everything on credit
and losing money even worse
every time I do so.
I just ignore my bank account
And keep paying on plastic
Keeping myself afloat with just
the credit I carry.
My bad habits worsen
And I continue to use it as if it'll last forever.
But credit has limits
And I have limits
And I know that eventually I'll have to stop.
I'll have to keep rebuilding and paying back
The bad habits I keep indulging.
I just swipe until I can't swipe anymore
Until I get rid of the credit line I have
because I'm desperate for something to make me
feel alive.
But it's all hollow victories.
In the end I have nothing but a full credit card
A space I don't have access to anymore.
In the end I have nothing
and nothing has me.

Gamble

One hundred, two hundred, three hundred,
four—
I just keep hoping and throwing at it more.
The tantalizing promise of winnings
Giving me the illusion of new beginnings.
I don't stop, I just keep going
Until it's all my money I'm owing,
Until I can't let go of my addiction
Until there's nothing left but friction.
But every small win or big one besides
Keeps me going, acts like a bribe.
I just can't resist the bigger score
So I keep going, keep paying out more.
And every now and then I win big
Even in a system that's obviously rigged,
Even though my money keeps going away,
I still feel the need to play every single day.

Searching

There is something I look for
Silence in my heart searching
Hoping I could find the way
To find my home in life eventually
I do not know where home is
Where home will eventually be
What life will look like in a few years
Or whether searching leads to finding
I always wanted home to be
With someone important, someone I love
With the person who I could be myself with
But I don't know where that home is
Do I forget the changes and past?
Do I let go the flaws and the edginess?
Is it difficult to forgive when
All I want is peace?
Perhaps I should think about being alone
Living on my own
And finding home with me
Where I can find peace
What peace can I find
In a space where I feel lonely?
Without you there I don't know safety
Without you there I don't know security
Is that peace?
Is that what I am searching for?

Interlude

I echo through my life
Echo the strains of my heart
But I fear it isn't enough
For my heart to beat

I skip a beat
I feel some pain
The interruption to the strains
Even though I'm not alone

Your soul met mine
Your heart beat in time
I fear the conclusion
To this musical intercession

So I echo through my life
My heart skipping when it knows you
And I wait
For conclusion to this interlude

Tyrant

You're a tyrant
An overlord
A fascist to my heart

You think you own the narrative
Make the decisions
Take the choices in your control

You think your way
Is the only way
And you expect me to bend

But you're just a tyrant
A controlling bastard
Someone who holds the reins to this ride

You don't want what I want
And I bend to what you want
But you're just a tyrant who wants control

You won't even consider
My needs or desires
You just carry on being an overlord

If you could just bend
And meet me somewhere between
This harsh NO world and my flights of fancy

I just want you to say yes
But you won't even consider the option
So we stay in this place

We stay here in limbo
No changes lifting me out
And you won't bend

Because you're just a tyrant
Dictating how our relationship is
But never considering how it could be

Mirror

She doesn't know how to keep going
She fights with her mind every day
The world is small to her
Just the space between her ears

She stands at the mirror feeling the pain
The daily pain of waking up
She fights every day to stand there
But everyone gets tired sometimes

She goes about her day fighting
The thoughts intrusive in her head
The mindless anger and sinking dread
She fights every single day

Part of her wonders why
Should she keep going
Should she keep trying
Or will she quit when it matters most

Her heart isn't in it anymore
She can't always find the will to carry on
The world loud around her
The silence terrible in her mind

She's gotten used to the voices
Telling her to end it
To leave and never come back
But she's stronger than those voices

At least she's stronger than she was

She looks in the mirror and knows
She isn't the same person anymore
She hasn't forgotten how to keep going

In her heart I know she knows
I know she can't walk away
She's tired but she's too scared
The darkness beyond scares her worse

I know her heart is broken
But she knows it won't last forever
Staring at the mirror she feels it again
The loneliness of living

But I know she won't leave
I know she can't make that choice
Because I know her well
I know her heart

She has a reason to stay
She always has a reason to keep trying
But reasons don't last forever
So she stares at the mirror and tries

But I know what she really thinks
About why she doesn't want to stay
Because I know her
Because she is me

And I haven't found a way out
I haven't found a chance to escape this
I just keep thinking that she'll get away
Get away from me

But those changes don't happen
The chances don't show up
And she stays and stays
But will she ever get away

I wish I could say

insomnia

I find myself awake
In the middle of the night
In the most cliche sense of things
I find myself there

I stare at the ceiling thinking
Dreaming dreams awake
The sun over the horizon beaming
Waiting for sleep or dawn

The feelings have caught up to me
Filling me with new-found things
Making me think of you at 2 a.m.
Following the sleepless days

The bubbling sense of desire
Of aspiration of you
The depth of the feeling fuzzy within
As I lay awake staring

Forgot to let go long enough
I'm overwhelmed but in the best way
Feeling the joy of you within me
The surge of feelings growing

So I can't help but smile in the night
Smile at my helpless fate
That I've jumped and fallen again
That I openly choose this sleepless night

In Passing

I have no control of my thoughts
I am on a plane now
Drifting from place to place
Thinking of the seat I sat in across from you
Wondering where you are in this moment

I know you're thriving where you are
That life has given you a gift in a way
But here on this plane
I wish you were my seatmate
And we were going to Europe together

But I'm just going home
To a place where I think about you
To places where the echo of you still lingers
Where the world turns but I am anchored
And you are the chain holding me

So even here on this plane
I'm waiting for the thoughts to subside
Somehow I hoped being up here would
Help me escape the pull of you
But all my thoughts are about you here

You've given me a gift in passing
New life at the end of an old one
An injection of happy in the middle of the sad
And changed my trajectory to you
Without my consent or decision

I am transformed

The world changing around me too
My world changing
But I don't find it frightening
I find it joyful because of the presence of you

So we keep going to the end
I keep texting you
And you keep responding (thank you)
Because I'm in love with you
And I never expected this in passing

the beast

in a snap
in a moment
a shift of values
a change of desires
an awakening
a realization of the truth
a dream come to life
in just a heartbeat
in a flutter of ventricles
the beast came to life
it opened a lazy glowing eye
(it slept for too long really)
dare i say it changed me
or did i change it?
without a chance to change
we would never wake
and the beast awoke
it woke deep in me
reminding me
of what I could be
and who I could be
and how I could be
and why
all because of the beast
woken up and roaring now
a surging wave of feeling
no control
but why would i need it?
i am a child clinging to monkey bars
and my fingers are tired
i want to let go and fall

into the void of you
into the ocean of you
my fingers uncurl and i'm ready
i think i'm ready
to let the beast take me
to let go

digging deeper

panic
the fear consumes me
the fear comes back to me
circling around and repeating
time and again

i dug a hole
i jumped in
no one pushed me
i chose this
and i hate myself for it

i can't help myself
i need help
but i don't know how to stop
how to stop playing
and digging the hole deeper

i keep sitting in the bottom of this hole
and sometimes i get out
but mostly i just jump back in
and dig deeper
till i'm underground

i don't know what i'm going to do
the end is near for my funds
the money is nearly gone
the panic setting in
till there's nothing left

i pray

i hope
i fear and cry
and panic again
but nothing convinces me to stop

so i keep going
and keep playing
till i can't stop and won't stop
till the end is here
till the last penny is gone

routine

around and around
the story goes
the day repeats
again and again

morning comes
and coffee goes
the time continues
without an end

je suis malade
je ne sais pas
pourquoi
je n'aime pas ma vie

i have forgotten
most things
that won't live the life
and continue on

the story goes on
till the coffee is gone
and i move on
with my day

second job

contemplating as I sit
thinking as I think
wondering about the day's disappearance
wondering if I can get out of this place

I keep working and waiting
the world outside this place changing
and I keep on with my boredom
continuing in this place

but I need the money so I keep going
I live in this place sometimes
I uproot my world for spare change
so I can keep going about my life

but still I feel only boredom
when I sit here in this place
just waiting for something to happen
to change the daily pace

but life goes on and I go with it
and my six hours are done in the end
I leave with some sense of purpose
and not much left to give

filler

these chapters go on
I know where the story goes
but I need more pages
between here and there

I need to develop the story
the story that lives in my head
the story I can't quite forget about
the one where my character's led

I forgot how hard this process was
I forgot it from last week
when I last wrote the words to the page
and the last days of working were bleak

but I can't forget the future writing
I wrote it out anyway
I leave those pages to the side
and find a way to connect

the story is strong in my mind
but weak on the page this first time
I don't know how to forget them
the person created in line

but still I keep working on my pages
the pages I can't seem to quit
the power of passion within me
even though this writing is shit

Pictograms from the Mind

Story of a Breaking Heart

Our lives crossed in vain
the beginning of lover's pain
With hearts open and shut
away from life I must be but—
The wounded heart only takes so much.

I held your hand just once
and you resisted my touch
No broken heart perceived
what love failed to let me receive—
But I can't forget the last thing you said.

You thanked me for understanding
instead of me reprimanding
You thanked me for the space
instead of telling me to my face—
The way I should have left before.

How can I be so kind
to this one who broke my mind
When I tried to get the answer
you just silenced faster—
The heart I had beating for you.

Maybe one day soon
this will end in the middle of June
But instead of turning away
I drifted towards you that day—
After I had that dream.

See if I trust my dreams

after all of this it seems
Without going forward
we just drifted toward—
This lonely end.

Vermont

A fleeting thing
A mood combined
You're leaving soon
But for now
I'll be here
In this moment
Where
I love you

A whispered truth
A pre-broken heart
But I don't care
I continue on
As if all things
Continue on

A lasting impression
A touch on my lips
I remember you most
From that first
Awkward non-kiss
But still
I cherish
That moment

A few weeks
A few days
I still savor
The mess we made
The love affair
Summer gave

As if
It would be my
Last

A Last Goodbye
A see you soon
Even if I don't
See you soon
Even if this
Is everything
Still
I prefer it here
In this moment
Where
I love you

Between Ordinary Blandness

I tasted for a moment
what it would be
To love you and feel you
Feeling love for me.
A heady expression of
reverberating emotion;
A feeling of strength
that permeates me.
I would let go but
I choose not to so
That I could just
once find heady love.
The kind of love that
makes you think and
makes you blink and
makes you want to
Love again soon.
But the moment passed
and left me behind
and took me in to
Leave me out to dry,
But I still wouldn't
change a thing.
What would life be
if not for these moments
of trial and error
between
ordinary blandness?

Bite My Lip

I bite my lip
I stare at you
I don't even realize
it when I do
You talk to me
Can't hold it in
I find myself
Rambling again
I find myself
Questioning
Do you like me too
Or is this my thing?
You say you do
I've been burned before
So I act with caution
But I want you more
And all these feelings
Boiling inside me
I can't ignore
And I don't wanna be free
I want to dive in
And forget my fear
Just let go
And kiss you here
But I bite my lip
And I hold back
I don't know what to do
I don't know how to act

I held your hand

I reached for you
I took your hand
I don't even know if you knew how to react when
       I did
But I still held it
I walked with you
Our cadences slightly off beat because you're so
       much taller than me
He held my hand
But I held his first
And later I think about how different it felt to feel
       it
The fingers entwined
The thumbs holding
But still I would do it again if I could, if you
       would let me
I reached for you
You held my hand
You didn't wave me off though I bet you were
       taken off guard when I did
My fingers on your arm
My fingers on your wrist
I think about the softness of your skin and the
       feel of it in my mind
But I held your hand
And you held mine
For just a few steps and a few strides I felt like it
       was right
Till I let go
And you let go

And we walked to our separate cars but first we
    hugged
My lips on your neck
Your skin on my mouth
I felt for a moment what it would be like to kiss
    you
But you walked away
And I walked away
And that day was not the day I would find out
    what it is like to kiss your salty lips
But I held your hand
And you held mine
And that touch haunts me days and weeks after,
    even if we do it again

just once

i thought just once
i might be able to let go
of my feelings for you
i don't really want to though

i thought just once
i might be able to stop
feeling what i felt
when i looked at your face
but i couldn't, could i?

something about you
something about your spirit
changed me
and brought me joy
even knowing it would end as it does

i thought maybe just once
i might get a reprieve from
my already-heartbreak state of being
thinking that it might be normal
to let go of all the things i wish I had

but i let go of the only thing
the hope i thought i could live with
the broken hope that wouldn't last

around the corner
i might find another chance
even though i savor this one
i savor my feelings for you

Real

I've changed
I know I have
But I don't think I've changed that much
I still love too much, too personally, too readily
Maybe that is me
The real me
The one who doesn't care about getting hurt but
cares about the possibility
The one who dives in without hesitation and tries
to find love there

Hollow

I watch you walk away
I watch you go your own way
Hollow in my bones watching
Feeling the absence of you there

I remind myself over and over
I am fine with this, I promise
My heart can handle the heartbreak
My heart can handle you gone

But I forgot this hollowed out feeling
I forgot because it's been so long
The way the heart breaks again and again
Taking breath and the stability

I stand on shifting sands with you
As you leave and maybe don't come back
We're parting now but the way is open
Our paths diverge, but could they change?

So I wait and watch you leave
I wish you well though I wish you'd stay
But I like all things changes are inevitable
And I find myself letting go of the hollowness in
         me

Never

You were never mine
But my heart was yours
You were never my boyfriend
But I thought of you that way
You were never gonna stay
But I wanted to savor the time
You were never gonna be with me
But I hoped for it anyway
You were never gonna kiss me
But I thirsted for it anyway
You were never gonna Love me
But I loved you anyway

Financial Grip

Negative numbers
Haunt my money
I don't take care
I don't know how to see
The loss keeps going
My addiction keeps growing
Have I lost my mind or
Am I losing everything else?
Every time
I look at my account
I fear the negative
I feel the grip
Of money coming to get me
Or debt coming to swallow me
Like sticky claws pulling you down
Dragging you to the depths of money Hell
Where there is no escape
Could I be wiser
Change my poor habits
Or at least learn the good ones?
The haunting effect
Of negative numbers and
Loss of money
Pursues me to my grave
My money—nor me—will never behave

Vacation

away or the same
in jungle or in sun-flame
where people go when they aren't occupied
their occupations lets them try
to find the passion in far away fly
but without drive their passion stupefied

intrinsic value in
working wage min
but time is the true currency of all things
away with your salary
justifying indecency
the disrespect for time always stings

unable to live
without the security it gives
so we work and toil without a moment's reprieve
with disrespect high
and life passing by
do we have a choice but to get up and leave?

Frack-tured

Mind on meds on the mend
but pills peak and pass their potency
Without working and words of worth
life loses light like a lost love

Fracturing feelings and forward force
breaking back building bought with a book
or opening options outside the office
Therapy takes time to temper the thoughts

Research relying on ready-made realities
can't connect comprehension coping with change
stealing soul-sucking silence till silence subsides
doctoring difficulties driven by daily drills

And after all attempts at altering actions
uproot understanding under unshared untruths
Healing hovers hard to hold, help hesitates
Giving no grace and guarding gratitude's gift

Blinding Light

The world was burning
I kept my head down, earning
Inside I was yearning
Longing for a change, a reprieve from this
       darkness

He left me
Changes I couldn't see
Echoes seeking the free
From all the days when the darkness
       overwhelmed

Then you came
You weren't the same
I found myself in Cupid's aim
And suddenly in the dark there was the blinding
       light of you

I don't think you know
How far I was ready to go
What darkness had started to grow
Before I found in my heart this feeling for you
       within me

I take your hand
On mine, no more wedding band
But alone I won't be and
I've found a way to see the beauty in the darkness
       again

It won't last

You'll eventually be the past
But I fell for you a little too fast
Looking for something, I found you here in
        blinding light

work

the hustle
the bustle
the split second decision
the change in the day
the life around me
I work and I figure
the work won't change me
but the work does change me
it changes me and how I live
the daily grind
the routine
the blind line of service I give
it eats away
at my guarded heart
the life I lead
has fallen apart
for money
for security
for financial win
I find myself waiting
for real life
to begin

change

a metamorphosis
a butterfly wing
a chance to live anew

a world beyond
a new leaf turned over
a metaphorical start

a crystalline flake
a hushed silence
a turning of the season

a flower bud
a feeling of renewal
a new day dawning

Redacted

Without Knowing

My heart it breaks in fields of joy
with nothing left to leave behind
But you are only being coy
with feelings spoken out in kind.
Here I hear your heart is breaking
on the eve of that one day
When we might finally stop the faking
of indifference when we stay.
"Indifference" that loathsome word
that keeps us loving but apart
I'd bet my life we'd be unheard
if we asked fate to unbreak this heart.
But really we just have us to blame
the onus on us again and again
And this one circumstance is same
as when we ended our love then.
I often question if the world
will once give us the joy we want
Or if the heart contracts, unfurled
and love remains a shameless taunt.
I've said it once and I say it here
that thing I feel and should believe
That even steeped in all this fear
I think you'll stay, that you won't leave.
When? you ask, and I ask too
but there aren't answers to this one
And without knowing I stay with you
choosing to trust when this limbo's done.

work in progress

frustrated
stuck and unable to move forward
the words won't come
the page is blank and unmoving
the story waits below the surface
and I can't get it out
the words won't come
I'm stuck repeating
just staring at the page and waiting
watching the cursor blink at me
the cursor that won't move
writing a letter then erasing
trying to find the inspiration
frustrated
the words won't come
I don't know how to express
I don't know how to find the words
I'm stuck and without a way forward
the story is stuck
and will I ever get the words out

Shoe Drops

I had been waiting
I had been feeling
I felt so many feelings
But this was by the worst

The other side of love—
A torment—
A trick of the mind
An illusion of kind
But I waded in fully aware
And now I'm stuck
Standing hip-deep
Waiting there

Did I love you?
Did I have time to figure that out?
Vanished like the mist in morning
Gone like the life I'm mourning
But without an answer to that supposition
Can I ever truly know the truth?

I know where you went and where you will be
But I know the onus is not on me
I know that I travel in my mind to see you
And that someday from you I'll finally be free

But for now I'm trapped
In this place where the other shoe drops
Where the abounding truth comes
Crashing down over me
Like waves come crashing in the sea

But I am burned again and again
No cooling water touches my skin
No reprieve I find from the end of this
I can't help but be lost and dismissed

I forget how to go and leave myself
Leave behind this feeling
Leave this toggle on my heart
But I know the torment is a part
The other side of love I find
The other side without you behind

Shedding

tears falling down
shedding away from my skin
shedding layers of pain from within
letting go of the hope I had

a waterfall of unjust truth
(unjust to me and maybe my truth)
but I find myself alone again
severed from that joy I lived

steady comes the fall
steady comes the salty sea
and the love that quenched in me
the doubt and despair, I set me free

I scratch my skin
I lose layers of me
setting loose the lost life
destroying the possibility of being fine

shed the layers
shed the expectations
shed the truth
but I cannot let go the truth

even with the truth abounding
and your soul rebounding
and my life unbounding
the hurt is resounding

I break away

shed skin behind me
someday I'll let go
of you and this place

deaf to the pleas
of my breaking heart
deaf to the truth
I am shredded apart

for all the things
I thought I knew
shedding was not
what I expected of you

so I flounder
I stumble
I fall and find footing
in this end I'm forgetting

Expectation

You said you couldn't be
what I needed of you
what I wanted of you
what you thought I wanted from you

You assumed what I wanted
what I never said I needed
that the connection of mind
would not be enough

Am I right in thinking
my expectations are sinking
that I am forgetting
the way to get out

Expectations just trap us
into linear thinking
and alcohol drinking
but not letting go

Am I lying to myself
when I say I don't expect
anything from you
anything at all?

Could I just be assuming
that I know what I want
when I feel something different
something I can't confront?

Screw Up

I messed up
I screwed up
Again (of course)
What else did you expect?

I did this to myself
One more time
Likely not the Last
But feels like it's passed

Do you understand?
Do you know why?
Or am I predictable
Repeating my lies?

I forgot all the lessons
The things I learned last time
The promises I let go of
To keep my heart kept

My life has changed
But this pattern remains
I screwed up this time
And I'm sure I will again

But the truth remains
This time isn't the same
Because *you're* not the same
And neither am I

So I carry on

Repeating the lie
That this is the Last
Screw up of my life

Limbo

I sit here waiting
The world turning below me
The procession of things passing me by
But I can't quite get to tomorrow
Stuck as I am in today
The world turning below me
The rest of life streaming past as I wait
Wait for the next thing to come
For a diagnosis that could come
For something that could change my life forever
But I am here
In this place
The world turning below me
While I sit here waiting
And I don't know how to keep going
To hold it together in this space
To let myself be a part of this world
And still find a path forward
The world turning below me
As I hover and wait
As I sit here waiting
For the diagnosis to come

Where'd You Go

slipped through my fingers
slipped through my grasp
as if my fingers
were made of broken glass

i felt you go
i felt it was the last
chances fade
and melodies pass

you told me i was too much
that i needed too much
that i take up too much energy
too much space for you

you told me that i
can't be your
priority
i guess that's true

you told me i want
more energy than you could give
more anything than you could give
but what about me

i poured my energy into you
for a fleeting moment or two
for a chance to capture love again
and feel the changes within my skin

and that's the catch, isn't it?

the heartbreak is real
because the love was real
just for a moment

infatuation passed
and reality came
but the more i knew you
the more i craved

you left me standing
holding the phone
without any semblance
of being un-alone

and still i know
i'd repeat it again
i gave up my solitary
existence for this

but you don't believe
that i'm worth the time
so these tears that i cry
are my companion tonight

hurt

abrasive
hurtful
unintentional?
i'm not sure

just abrasive
and blunt
like you wanted me to be
like you wanted you to be
so that you could
test me

safe
unsafe
you said you feel
with yourself
but i know
i can deal

give
or take
space for you
so that you can let go
so that i can be me
and let you go

grasping
just grasping
at straws every time
i know you don't see it
you don't hear this rhyme

because i don't
share it

cry
uncry
for reasons unknown
or maybe known
my heart beats again
for the thing
i have
lost

pain
so demur
to be heartbroken
again
without so much
as a glimmer
of friend

speaking
silence
respecting fables
i tell myself
to cajole
my impulse

release
relinquish
the phone
and the communication as well
let go of the words
let go this spell

abrasive
just abrasive
the bluntness you gave
you've taken away
the one thing
i crave

again

heartbroken again
wow, like you're surprised
we've been here before
i'm sad in your eyes

heartbroken again
as if i can ever win
as if i can be myself
and still find love

heartbroken again
like i live for this
like i want this
like i ask for this

heartbroken again
funny, it feels like karma
but it shouldn't be
no love should be

heartbroken again
perhaps this is the last?
i don't know if i want it
i feel stupid to let it pass

the chase

I keep avoiding
I keep ignoring
You keep me at arm's length while I pursue you
       and love you
My heart breaks
My soul feels you
You don't know the depths of my feelings for you
I keep chasing
I keep feeling
You know I'm chasing but not what I'm feeling
       though I should say something
My desire grows
My inhibition fades
One day it'll collapse and I'll kiss you like I've
       wanted to since day one
I found you
I dreamt of you
You came to life in front of me, and I can't seem
       to leave

hello, goodbye

where did I go
where did you go
I know where you went
but I went nowhere

you left with your dreams
and your enchanted themes
and all the things
that keep you going

I stood by
and watched you fly
watched you chase
your world of tomorrow

I can't stand back
and express the lack
of hurt because
there was too much to bear

but when did you leave
when my heart did grieve
with the world behind me
telling me I'm fine

I won't be fine
not this time
I'll carry on anyway
I'll carry the torch

how did I fall
without prelude or call
with my heart leading me
down a path I won't know

with beauty in my sight
and your long goodnight
I wish I could love you
like I love the idea of you

but you're long gone
and my heart carries on
till our paths cross again
on the other side of your dreams

Wicked

I am a wicked woman
a woman who dreams of dark things
a woman with darkness inside of her
dreaming of destroying all things

I am a wicked woman
who looks with evil in her eye
desiring to take out the world's laughter
by punching the Man in the eye

I am a wicked woman
suppressed by my own accord
holding back from expressing my violence
violence I cannot afford

I am a wicked woman
a woman with self-control
without my holding-back strength
I'd bury myself in a hole

I am a wicked woman
I forge my own wicked path
I let go the world's conventions
I scream to let go my wrath

I am a wicked woman
you cannot handle my power
I live my life beyond the boundaries
of the world's final hour

I am a wicked woman

I have forgotten how to live
the darkness still surrounds me
I have nothing left to give

Hospital

i am blind but i still see
one eye is blind but the other is free
i feel the fear of loss and strain
of change upon my brain
i forgot the fear of unknowing

i am here but i am not
i am in a place that must be forgot
the food is plain, the bed is fine
i am not here to sleep or dine
the world goes on without me stuck as i am

they visit me at all hours
the ones with white coats and medical powers
the ones who draw blood from my hand
the ones who will never understand
that the ones i want to visit are not here to offer
        comfort

the voices silent in my phone
texting to tell me I'm not alone
so I won't feel so isolated here
and that I feel there is nothing to fear
but it doesn't matter because i still feel like i'm on
        my own

Broken

Secrets finding their way out of my heart
I hold on to them but they slip through my grip
My fingers feeling the brush of them
As they fly away again

Chiming in on my own opinion
I find my silence to be repugnant
I wait for secrets coming back to me
As they always seem to do

I listen to sad music and just hold on
I find my way through the tangle of secrets
Hoping to let go of them eventually
To speak then into existence

Some are inevitable to share
Some are mine and some are not
But I keep my grip the same
Letting them slip through

But I forgot how crazy this life could be
And how hard it is to hold on
To anything much less secrets
So I let go

I speak the truths I've coveted
I open my fingers and let them go
Secrets I guarded to keep others at bay
But I let my guard down

My only chance for redemption

Close my fists again
But I've forgotten how
And I don't want to anymore

There has to be a reason

WHY
Why can't I just find a normal one
No NOT normal
Someone who is well-adjusted
Or able to take care of themselves
Someone not looking for a caretaker

Why can't I find someone
Who takes care of themselves
Who find their inner strength
Instead of finding outer strength
Who holds on

I just want someone to be supportive
Instead of being supported all the time
I feel like I never find that
Even when the illusion is there
They pretend to be for my sake

In the end the truth always outs
Their inner weakness never subsides
They never seem to be strong enough to be mine
But they're not mine
They never were

I chose not to make them mine

Why can't I find someone I would choose
A thousand times choose
A million times
Without hesitation or reservation

Without a moment of doubt

But that's not how it goes
We never find anyone like that
Like the dream of a well-adjusted love
Someone who takes care of themselves
So that we can take care of we

As if the world doesn't believe in
A person like that
Why do I still bother
To seek and never find
Why does it have to be like this

Can we just find each other and move on?

Sad songs

The sad strains keep me from ignoring it
The tune reminds me of what I've felt
I feel the tears and the jangle of my soul
The music taking its toll on me

The reminder is enough to kill me
I feel the power of past feelings overwhelming
Drowning me in a stifling remembrance
Deafening my soul's hearing
Till all that's left is the memory

Tiger waiting in the grass
The sounds of sad songs waiting in my
          headphones
In silence lurks the sad song strains
Waiting for the moment to strike

When I let my guard down I find myself given
Handing myself to the pain of the reminder
I cannot escape these sad songs of love
And I actively choose to listen

Why do I do this to myself
Hearing and listening to these sad sad songs
Pummeling myself with the constant reminder
Of things gone by that would never last

The trill of memory settles down on me
I turn off the music and forget to remember
But I don't wait long till I turn back the music

I'd rather feel pain and remember than forget you
again

Now 23

He was only 22 now 23
He left me here holding my heart
Now don't hurt me
I forgot the language of love never speaks without
      metaphor

We met a long time ago
He was off my radar then
I liked him but didn't fall for him
Yet
That would come later as it usually does

That summer was his last to be here
I forgot about the feelings that could creep up on
      me
I forgot about the way falling happens
So I forgot I could dream about the one I love

And that's how it happened of course
I had a dream in which we spoke Italian
And in which I kissed him
So I longed to know that in the waking hours

From that dream I realized
I liked him more than I realized
And every day he walked through the door
I brightened just a little bit

So I didn't think I just acted
I asked him for coffee
Not realizing that I was asking him *out* for coffee

Until a few minutes later
But he said yes of course
What did I have to worry about?

That first time going out
Just for coffee
I almost kissed him when we were leaving
I regret that now
Not taking that chance
Because I really wanted to
But I chickened out

I told you that in a text later
You gave me hope then
My heart pounded in response

We met again for dinner this time
I held your hand more than once
I know it wasn't the most natural thing for you
I know how hard it is to be comfortable with that
But we walked and I almost kissed you again
Instead I kissed your neck
I could taste your skin for hours afterward

I fell for you somewhere around then
I fell harder than I intended to
But every time I saw you it didn't wane
And I didn't shy away from it
I'm no longer scared of falling
Or of heartbreak

I knew you would break my heart
I knew it would happen inevitably

You were leaving for school
For New England
For a place so far we wouldn't see each other for
        a long time

My heart undone before I even fell
My soul crushed before I could even hope
I carried on hoping that something good will
        come of it
Though I knew the best I could do is fall and get
        hurt

Then August happened
And I ended up in the hospital
And you came to see me
You just made me love you more
By then I can say I did

The last time we were to get dinner
I ended up in the hospital again
You picked me up and dropped me off there
And I said goodbye to you
Because you were leaving

I went to kiss you
But you pulled away
I sighed inside and didn't try again
I said see you later and I left
And then you left a couple days later

My heart broke for you

And I still miss you more

We still talk sometimes
But I don't have the hope I once did
Because you were 22 now 23
And I know the boundaries there
I know the obstacles to a love like this

I want to see you happy and healthy
With someone you've fallen for as I fell for you
I want you to thrive in your newfound life
Because I love you
More than you probably know

So I carry on loving you from afar
You in your New England home
Me in my Mid-Atlantic dwelling
Everything as it should be

Frozen

I feel so cold now
So detached from everything
Like the heart in me is empty
A shell of what I used to be
Numbness clutches me
A feeling of insecurity of emotion
How do I wake up from this slumber?
How do I wake up from this sleep?
I don't connect anymore
With the things that used to awaken in me
The emotional response of tears or fears
Or love from which I fight to survive
The scars of memories still trace my mind
Lines of red across the dark sky
Fears that I'll never get back to who I was
Live in me and eat away at my peace of mind
But I forget to feel again
I think instead of letting the tears come
And I'll never know again the rush of emotion
I let go of everything but the numbness within
But still sometimes I catch the glimmer
The coldness thaws for just a moment
And I forget to be detached
Instead giving myself space to react
But then I close myself off again
And force myself to let go of emotion
And sink back down into the frigid waters
And sink back down into the arctic of me

always say

I think you know
I think you know how much
You hurt me
When you always say
"We're not boyfriend and girlfriend"

I think you know
How much it hurts
When you always say
You want
Personal s p a c e
Away from me

You always say
You love me
You always say
You want a future with me
But I don't believe you
Anymore

I think you know
How much that hurts
And how hard it is to be
Your temporary solution
To loneliness

But you always say
I love you
And I believe you
And I love you too

But is love enough?
MM says
"Love is not enough"
And I believe MM too

And I bend over backwards for you
For your personal s p a c e
And I feel like I do the right thing
All the time
By staying away when you don't want me
But where is my reprieve?
Where is my apology
For calling me your girlfriend
When you don't mean it?
For asking for space when I'm in pain
For taking away my pillar of strength
When I need it most?

But you always say
I'm in the wrong
When all I'm asking
Is to be important to you
When all I want
Is to be your wife
But you don't want that life
You don't want me that way
You just want the fun
Not the c o m m i t m e n t
Just the passing moments
The romanticized dating
Not the real stuff
The hard stuff

Just the frosting
Not the cake

But that's not enough for me
Not anymore
Not ever if I'm honest
But you always say
Just friends
When I want this friendship to
End
And progress further
You don't want that
The growth and pain
That comes with "Fuck yes"
But if I'm honest
You're no longer a
"Fuck yes"
Because you always say
What we're not

But I think you know
How much it hurts
Every time you always say

messaging

flutters in my stomach
I feel the sensation closing in
nerves begin to take hold
and it's all because of you

the sound of your dedicated ringtone
the sight of a message from you
sends a thrill through me
my stomach trembles within

but what does the message say?
I'm driving but I read it anyway
you can't stop me, you're not here
so I open it and half-read it

electricity buzzes through me
the words quickening my heartbeat
my soul waking up
leaping out of me with every syllable

the words entrance me
I find myself unfocused, still driving
lost in my thoughts of you
and I forget to text you back

soft secrets

I am quiet
I hold the thoughts in
I hold myself from the truth

I forget the sound of honesty
The secrets inside never spilling out
The silence a comforting blanket

I wear armor against my truth
I wear the pain of not speaking
Because in truth I want to speak

But I don't always tell the truth
I hold back
I hold it in

The grin of apathy follows me
The feeling of unfeeling preventing me
From speaking again

I am torn apart by this sensation
And I should break away from this habit
But I can't and I won't

I forget what is real and what is not
I forget to speak the truth
I forget when I speak to you

Late Formalism

Falling

Autumn of my life
Falling in Love one more time
Golden light of hope
A reprieve from the darkness
You captured me once again

in the cold

Winter on my mind
The crispness of your absence
The warmth around me
Falters without you by me
Come be my blanket tonight

dichotomy

You are my night star
I am the moon in the sky
Apart we shine bright
Together we shine brighter
The darkness recedes from us

You are my tall tree
I am the fall leaf drifting
The wind carries me
Circling you in our fall dance
Letting go of what once was

You are my bell tone
I am the bell still ringing
The echo of you
Resonates within my soul
Reminding me of time past

You are my springtime
I am the winter's chill gone
The first sign of spring
The bud opening bringing
New light to our turning year

Light

The glimmer of you
The way your soul shines brightly
Guides me on my way
Gifting me the path I sought
And a way forward with you

NSFW

The touch of your skin
Electricity between
Skin to skin as one
Hours passing as seconds
I find my heaven with you

I dig my hands in
Twist the sheets in my fingers
Twist my body too
Until the bed is undone
And I am undone as well

Sweat upon my brow
My body weak but also strong
Soul flying from me
Till I find bliss in your arms
Till I see heaven with you

this moment

I run to your arms
I find myself craving you
Your skin on my skin
Is where I would choose to be
I live for these brief moments

You're only here now
Soon you'll be leaving again
But for now you're here
Resting in my warm embrace
Resting in my sheets with me

You remind me of
The person I want to be
The person I am
And the person I love most
You are the one I love most

I run to your arms
Let go of inhibition
Forget all my fears
And run to you ready for
This moment to never end

the reminder of you

The wind blows chilly
The sky fills with wispy clouds
The night is gone now
The day is coming on strong
I hold still in thoughts of you

Leaf falling from branch
Flower's chilly bloom ending
Grass rustling in wind
The echo of birdcall beckons
I wait silent as winter

Scarlet lights above
Sunlight on mirrored windows
Green lights glow below
Filtered streetlight yellow-white
I see you in city lights

Swish of car passing
Crunch of gravel on the road
Horns reverberate
Even traffic makes music
I think of you as I wait

Helicopter flies
Truck chugs along hurriedly
Commuters run fast
Catching trains in underground
I listen for your music

turning

summer's kiss is gone
the setting of summer's sun
autumn waits to come
the winter's taken over
pushing aside the warm days

chronos

I need more time now
Time to live in the moment
Time to save for then
So I can find my way through
This holding space I'm trapped in

Tick tock tick tock tick
I hear the temporal click
The way the time passed
Going forward to the end
The change has come back again

I break away now
From the life I have sewn here
Drifting once again
Unanchored and swimming free
Till the shore meets me again

Then I wait for change
Or the current on the seas
To take me away
From this grey empty shoreline
Away from this wild expanse

Still time trickles on
Going to places unseen
Till I see the world
I'm alone on the ocean
I'm a buoy drifting free

notification

endorphins run high
capturing my attention
running me ragged
until I'm gasping for air
until I can't turn away

my cellphone lights up
another endorphin rush
a hit to my brain
and a waiting game again
waiting for the next message

too much time passes
I don't get the endorphins
I crave your message
lighting up my phone again
calling me awake from sleep

but still the silence
carries on and on and on
while I wait again
until the silence deafens
and I can't wait anymore

finally a note
a message comes through again
but I don't care now
I've waited too long for you
apathy sets in once more

back to me

I thought you were gone.
I thought this journey ended.
But you came right back,
The old adage proving true,
What you let go will return.

I let go of you
I felt it best to do so.
Just let you go on,
Moving on in your full life,
Living where you would excel.

You went on to thrive,
To live your best self again,
And I felt so glad
You found the place you belong
Even if it's far from me.

You came back to me,
In words if not in action.
You returned to me
Reminding me of your soul
And all the emotions there.

You came back to me
I thought you were gone for good.
I thought it would be
A long time till I see you
Till your hand is in my hand.

I feel excitement,
Anticipation over
Your soon arrival.
I can't wait to look you in
The eye as you look in mine.

I wait for return,
Impatiently if I'm honest,
I feel your presence,
I feel you on my fingers
I feel you though you're not here.

Your soul's reflection
A golden light in my eyes
Reminding me of
The first time I fell for you
The overwhelming feeling.

You came back to me,
You send a thrill through my soul.
I had forgotten
But you came back, now I know
I could never let you go.

This is not the end

This is not the end.
Endings are just beginnings
By another name.
I walk this path with you
And find the beginning here.

I sleep soundly now,
Secure in the knowledge of
Your professed love of
Me and I let go again,
Jump without a parachute.

The summer ended,
I left my feelings back there
In the heat of June.
August took you far away,
The chill of autumn kept you.

But I sleep soundly,
The bracing cold of winter
Brings you on your way
Back to this place where I fell,
Back to August heat again.

And I learned again
That ends don't really end
Ends begin again;
This time with gusto for you,
This time with your hand in mine.

Alone

I was fine alone.
I was living my own way.
I knew myself and
All I wanted and my dreams.
I lived my truth by myself.

This was how I lived.
Alone but not alone if
You count all my friends.
I knew what I wanted then,
I knew my own self and me.

Then the floor gave out.
My world tumbled into
A cacophony,
Rocking what I thought I knew,
Sending me flying again.

And at the bottom,
Somewhere far below the floor,
I fell into you.
Out of the cacophony
Order that is your bell tone.

I was fine alone.
But why be fine when you can
Fly on wings of sound?
The warm tones of you take me
Away from this loneliness.

Forget

I forgot your face.
I forgot the light of you.
I forgot the past,
I forgot everything too.
I forgot to forget you.

I travelled with you,
I carried you in my heart.
I took you with me.
I waited for your return.
I break my heart with waiting.

ABOUT THE AUTHOR

Breska Liotson is an incidental poet who stumbled into the artform at age eleven. Though her work has matured since then, she still looks back on those poems fondly as an early expression of some then-important topics.

Her previous publications include *The Silence of My Mind*.

She lives on the east coast with her tenacious cat.

www.ingramcontent.com/pod-product-compliance
Lightning Source LLC
Chambersburg PA
CBHW021130020426
42331CB00005B/708